Original title:
A Home Full of Green

Copyright © 2025 Creative Arts Management OÜ
All rights reserved.

Author: Vivian Laurent
ISBN HARDBACK: 978-1-80581-737-6
ISBN PAPERBACK: 978-1-80581-264-7
ISBN EBOOK: 978-1-80581-737-6

Unity in the Embrace of Nature

In the corner a cactus sits,
With a hat that just won't quit.
The dog stares with a puzzled glance,
Wondering if it's time to dance.

The curtains sway with leafy cheer,
As a squirrel scampers near.
The cat thinks she owns the show,
While the ferns get too much glow.

We've got plants that seem to laugh,
And a rubber tree that's quite a calf.
The goldfish seems to plot and scheme,
While the sunlight sips its cream.

In this jungle of playful mess,
Even gnomes don their Sunday best.
Together we swing and sway,
In our garden of quirky play!

The Solace of Sage and Sunlight

In the kitchen, herbs have grown,
They plot a heist for all I've sown.
Sage and thyme have formed a band,
Together, they wage a leaf-filled stand.

The sunlight spills, a golden spill,
My plants demand I pay the bill.
They whisper tales with crinkled leaves,
A garden circus, oh how it believes.

Bright daisies dance with oversize hats,
While cheeky snails have races with the cats.
The carrots whistle in the softest breeze,
As I trip over weeds, down on my knees.

With each sprout, my heart does sing,
Who knew these greens would grant me bling?
From herbs that jest to blooms that jest,
This greentopia surely beats the rest.

Nature's Quilt of Tranquility

Underneath the shady tree,
Nature stitched a quilt for me.
With patches bright, and colors bold,
It's where my secrets are retold.

The flower beds, a jumbled mess,
Stand up tall like a wild dress.
They hide my snacks, oh what a lark,
I find a donut, then a spark.

The frogs croak tunes that crack a smile,
While bees throw parties, just for a while.
The grass keeps growing—what a tease!
I mow it down, then curse and sneeze.

Each walk reveals a brand new game,
In my green haven, nothing's the same.
A squirrel grabs my sandwich quick,
In this wild scene, I just can't pick!

The Green Canvas of our Lives

Canvas blooms, it's quite a sight,
A palette lush, from day to night.
Paintbrush petals, colors so bright,
Art in the garden, what pure delight.

Gumdrop blossoms, they twist and sway,
Telling jokes in their own gay way.
The daisies giggle, the roses grin,
Each plant's a character, let's begin!

Hedgehogs roll by with berry treats,
While sunflowers lean on their tiny seats.
A butterfly winks with flair and style,
Together we laugh, all the while.

Pollinators buzz in a fervent race,
Each little critter knows its place.
In this green world, life's a show,
Crafting joys wherever we go.

Garden Tales of Resilience

Once there was a bean so stout,
Told tales of triumph, no doubt.
With roots that laughed, it grew so high,
A green superhero, oh my, oh my!

Beside it squatted a lazy gnome,
Dreaming loudly of his far-off home.
But every time the weathers grow,
He finds new ways to steal the show.

The radishes wiggle, red and round,
With puns about what's underground.
While carrots tell stories down below,
"Next week we'll have a veggie show!"

Spring rains come and they dance the jig,
While cabbages boast they're the biggest gig.
In this patch where resilience thrives,
With each silly plant, laughter survives.

Nurtured by Foliage and Light

In a jungle of socks and tangled vines,
Cats chase dust motes, ignoring our signs.
Potted plants giggle, swaying for fun,
While dishes pile high, their wash-cycle run.

A salad in the fridge, half-chewed by mice,
Promising greens turn to veggie-shaped dice.
The sunlight streams in, like a giant tickle,
As we dance with the ferns, oh what a fickle!

Living room vines, they twist and they twirl,
Caught in the blender of life's wild whirl.
We trip on the petunias, a colorful sight,
In this leafy ballet, we chaotically delight.

Watering cans sing with each rhythmic splash,
While squirrels peek in, looking for cash.
Involving each creature, not one left behind,
In this messy, green haven, pure joy we find.

Green Dreams in Every Corner

Things sprout in the oddest of places,
Droopy plants making funny faces.
The fridge hums songs of forgotten greens,
A kaleidoscope garden of bizarre scenes.

Up on the shelf, a fern named Fred,
Claims to be king, "I'm better than bread!"
With wispy leaves high, he holds court with glee,
Beneath him, a cactus shouts, "What about me?"

A salad of socks strewn across the floor,
Nature's errant children behind every door.
Green dreams oozing from every nook,
As we stumble through like a wacky storybook.

Pictures hang crooked, art made of weeds,
"Our life's an adventure!" the plant party leads.
Whimsical wonders grow taller each day,
In this quirky abode, the plants steal away.

The Leafy Oasis of Quietude

In corners where silence is seldom seen,
Lurking leaf monsters lurk, crafty and lean.
They whisper strange secrets, rustling so loud,
Claiming the chamomile tea draws a crowd.

Silly vines dodge under our feet like pro,
Gentle reminders that they steal the show.
Mossy green carpets soften each fall,
While potted mischief waits, daring us all.

Cozy corners where sunlight spills,
Giggling plants rattle their chlorophyll thrills.
A parrot named Chuck thinks he runs the place,
Chasing off shadows with a colorful grace.

Laughter erupts—oh, what a scene!
In this leafy haven, we're all living green.
Shenanigans grow wild, the air filled with cheer,
In the leafy embrace of our tender frontier.

Rooted Reveries of Belonging

Around every table, the ferns have their say,
Bamboos crack jokes in a green cabaret.
A mismatched ensemble of snickers and leaves,
In this colorful chaos, everyone believes.

Roots dancing below, tangled and free,
Feeding the dreams of our botanic spree.
Dandelions frolic while sunflowers sigh,
In this playful patch, we all wave goodbye.

Painted leaves gossip like best friends at noon,
As we trip over pots, swaying to a tune.
An ivy creeps up and takes on the lead,
Spinning wild tales where none would concede.

Barking dogs marvel at the hanging herbs,
While laughter rings out, our joy it disturbs.
In our rooted revelry, life leans in tight,
Filling the air with a whimsical light.

Echoing the Wind's Green Song

Leaves giggle as they sway,
In a dance that's light and gay.
Squirrels argue on their spree,
Chasing tails, so wild and free.

Sunbeams play hide and seek,
A cheeky game, so unique.
Grass tickles toes that roam,
Every patch feels like home.

Birds sing quirky little tunes,
Crowning branches, mocking moons.
Crickets chirp in their delight,
Laughing at the starry night.

Nature's voice, a merry band,
Echoes through this vibrant land.
Even frogs croak jokes in beats,
In this laughter, life repeats.

Hearthstone surrounded by Hyacinths

At the hearth, the flowers grin,
In their pot, a wild din.
Petals blush; they love the heat,
Swapping tales of life so sweet.

Daisies whisper in the breeze,
"I've got pollen, wanna tease?"
While tulips flash their colored hats,
Competing with the cheeky cats.

Beneath the stove, a secret radish,
Too shy to leave, it's gotten lavish.
Cooking up plans for a feast,
With veggies who love to say the least.

Mirth fills every bloom and petal,
Jokes flying like a wild metal.
In this patch of colors bright,
Laughter grows with pure delight.

Eden's Enchantment in Every Room

In the kitchen, herbs conspire,
Whispering recipes of fire.
Basil rolls its eyes in charm,
While thyme spreads warmth with no alarm.

Cacti wear their prickly shoes,
Inviting all to sing the blues.
A fern pretends it's quite the star,
Gesturing wildly from afar.

In the den, a rubber plant,
Dances with a lively chant.
Stories shared through leafy tales,
While laughter bursts, and joy prevails.

Windows open to the scene,
Of playful critters on the green.
Every corner hums a tune,
As nature dips beneath the moon.

Flourish in Every Fissure

Cracks in walls, a green parade,
Tiny plants in rogue charade.
"Look at me, I sprouted here!"
Said the weed, full of cheer.

Underfoot, a timid sprout,
Whispers secrets throughout.
"Who needs space?" it shouts with glee,
"I'll thrive where you can't see me!"

Vines snake up the old stone stairs,
Chasing sunlight, unaware of cares.
A blooming chaos, of pure charm,
Each petal wears a winning arm.

Even shadows seem to grin,
In this mix of thick and thin.
Life insists on breaking through,
With humor in a vibrant hue.

Life's Palette of Flora

In the garden, veggies dance with glee,
Tomatoes blushing, feeling quite free.
Carrots wearing shades, oh what a sight,
While cucumbers giggle, all through the night.

Sunflowers gossip, with their heads held high,
Peas in their pods, all wondering why.
Bees buzzing jokes, their humor so sweet,
Telling the daisies, 'You're really quite neat!'

Echoes of Leaves and Laughter

Leaves that chuckle in the gentle breeze,
Whispering secrets among the trees.
The squirrels are plotting their acorn heist,
While birds serenade, 'Come join the feast!'

Rabbits in pajamas, stashing their greens,
Rolling on the grass, in the sun's bright beams.
Every fern and flower joins in the fun,
Nature's great circus, out under the sun.

Verdant Pathways Within

Stepping through grasses, tickling my toes,
Trusting the soil, where the wildflower grows.
A path lined with dandelions so bold,
Says, 'Life is a party, come join, be sold!'

Licorice stems sway to the tune of delight,
While mushrooms are dancing, oh what a sight!
Frogs sing their solos beneath the moon's beam,
In this forest of laughter, where all creatures dream.

Green Tapestry of Everyday

In every corner, leaves peek and play,
Cacti wear hats, it's shrubbery day!
The mint stand-up crew, so witty and spry,
Tickling our senses, they never run dry.

The garden's a stage, with acts all around,
A rose with a joke, and its thorns make a sound.
Life's bright hues dance on this banquet of glee,
As laughter takes root, and joy grows like a tree.

Echoes of the Wild in Every Room

Tiny creatures roam the floor,
Their tiny paws, a soft encore.
A squirrel in pajamas leaps,
While copper pots hold secrets deep.

The cat debates with leafy friends,
A duel that never seems to end.
Laughter hides in every nook,
As plants reply with each new look.

In the bathroom, ferns discuss,
Who has the best shampoo? Who's fussed?
Cactus in the corner quips,
'You're all just jealous of my tips!'

A wild chorus fills the space,
Where nonsense reigns and goblins race.
Echoes dance with joy, sincere,
In this green circus, loud and sheer.

Shades of Green in Sunshine and Rain

Greens that giggle in the light,
Whispering tales both day and night.
Moss wears slippers, oh so grand,
While ivy plays in rock bands.

When the rain starts, leaves do a dance,
Singing in droplets, taking a chance.
Puddles form a splashy floor,
Where frogs hold concerts, never a bore.

Sunshine wraps the room in cheer,
While shadows wink and disappear.
Cabbage patches join in the fun,
Declaring every day a pun.

'Look at us!' the greens proclaim,
'In every shade, we spread our fame!'
Nature wears a brilliant crown,
Making every frown fall down.

The Patina of Nature's Artistry

Painted leaves in vibrant hues,
Swirl and twirl in leafy shoes.
Lettuce sketches on the wall,
While broccoli holds the curtain call.

Twisted vines tell stories bold,
Of garden parties long foretold.
The sunbeams laugh, the shadows play,
In nature's art, we roam and sway.

Sculptures grow where soil meets care,
Charming gnomes with cheeky flair.
Every corner filled with jest,
A gallery that never rests.

When plants can party, who would doubt?
They play the flute, swing all about.
So grab a brush, let colors fly,
In this gallery, we'll never shy.

Abode of the Verdure Dreamers

In the quirky halls, plants conspire,
To plot a joke, to set afire.
A hanging fern plays peek-a-boo,
While sleepy vines claim night's hue.

Pillows stuffed with moss and dreams,
Fluffy as clouds, bursting seams.
Worms debate what soil fits best,
In this abode, they take their rest.

Windows dressed in leafy lace,
Where ladybugs have found their place.
The sunbeam dances on the floor,
Inviting all to laugh and roar.

So here we dwell, with greens galore,
Plant pals and laughter to the core.
In every leaf, a tale unfolds,
In a world where silliness holds.

A Nest Beneath the Fronds

In a patch where ferns do sway,
A squirrel thinks it's here to stay.
He nests in leaves, a soft buffet,
And hosts his friends for lunch each day.

The snails parade like it's a show,
While worms wiggle low, still in tow.
The ants hold hands, in ranks they go,
To dance beneath the breezy glow.

A robin chirps, a little loud,
'This leafy spot's a modest crowd!'
The hedgehogs laugh, a merry shroud,
As nature's stage becomes endowed.

So here's a tale of leafy cheer,
Where critters gather year by year.
They toast with dew, and loud they cheer,
In fronds and greens, there's naught to fear.

Oasis of Color and Calm

A patch of daisies, waving wide,
Where ladybugs and laughter glide.
The grass grows long, a slip 'n slide,
For frogs who leap with froggy pride.

In sun's embrace, they pile up high,
A sloth swings slow, a sleepy sigh.
The tulips gossip, oh my, oh my,
While bees bring news with buzzing fly.

A rogue raccoon trips over roots,
With startled eyes in muddy boots.
He joins the party, laughing hoots,
As rabbits hop in silly toots.

The colors clash, a rainbow brawl,
Where chirps and squeaks blend in the thrall.
It's chaos wrapped in nature's call,
An oasis where we all stand tall.

Whispers of the Verdant Haven

Amidst the leaves, the whispers play,
A wisdom shared from tree to bay.
The kittens pounce in grand ballet,
While butterflies flaunt, what a display!

The pond reflects blue skies so proud,
While turtles bask beneath the cloud.
A squirrel's speech draws quite a crowd,
With tales of nuts and acorns loud.

The hedges sway with youthful glee,
As owls improve their comedy.
With cackles shared, so wild and free,
Their laughter rides the honey bee.

So linger long in leafy dreams,
Where sunlight spills in playful beams.
In this haven, nothing seems,
To stop the fun or quiet screams.

Sanctuary in the Leafy Embrace

In leafy arms, the world feels light,
Where giggles turn the day to night.
The flowers duke it out in flight,
As frogs on lily pads invite.

A raccoon eats cake, without a care,
While birds all judge, a feathered stare.
The wind blows softly through the air,
A comedy, the forest's fair.

The moles discuss their underground,
While textures change, with sights profound.
They wear their crowns without a sound,
In earthy jokes, the laughs abound.

So join the fray, embrace delight,
Where every green is bold and bright.
In this sanctuary, day or night,
Both nature's jest and humor's flight.

Vibrant Views from Every Window

Through the panes, a leafy show,
Squirrels dance, putting on a glow.
The birds chirp jokes, a feathered jest,
While I sip green tea, feeling blessed.

The garden gnomes take the lead,
With tiny shovels, planting seeds.
They argue over who's the best,
As I roll my eyes, quite unimpressed.

The sun peeks in, a playful tease,
Turning my sofa into a breeze.
The plants gossip, in their green spree,
I swear they're planning on a jubilee!

Each window scene's a circus act,
With leafy acrobats intact.
Who needs TV with this delight?
Nature's show is always bright!

Nature's Symphony Inside

A violin made of glowing vines,
Nature's orchestra, weird designs.
The wind plays flutes, the raindrops chime,
I hum along, not quite in time.

A grasshopper drums on the nearest pot,
While a frog croaks out a solo plot.
With twigs as sticks, the crickets score,
This isn't what I'd planned, for sure!

The daisies sway, assuming leads,
In a green gown with floral beads.
They tried to turn my chair into a throne,
But I prefer my squishy-zone.

Cacti chuckle, in their pointy way,
Saying, "Man, we've got all day!"
The earth hums low, a giggly beat,
With laughter growing beneath my feet!

The Quietude of Green Folly

In every corner, a blushing fern,
With a funny sense of humor to learn.
The pothos plants roll their eyes,
At my attempts to get them to rise.

An avocado pit claims it's a tree,
While the washing machine laughs at me.
A cheeky cactus gave me a poke,
As I told it jokes, thinking it woke.

The ferns whisper secrets, oh so sly,
While I trip over branches, oh my!
A jungle, yes, but most unkempt,
I never knew plants had such contempt!

In this green chaos, we all meet,
Bamboos snicker at my dancing feet.
With every step in this leafy scheme,
Life's just a funny, growing dream!

Aromas of Earth and Sap

The smell of moss, it steals the show,
With cookie crumbs that sprouts bestow.
Bees buzzing jokes, they laugh and twirl,
With nature's scents like a fragrant pearl.

I cooked a stew with garden thyme,
But now it's a plant party in prime.
Rosemary frowns at my cooking flair,
Saying, "This isn't how you prepare!"

Garlic chives are in on the fun,
They said, "Hey bud, this smells like a pun!"
Lemon balm giggles, "That's quite a dish!"
"Just add some nectar, and fill your wish!"

The earthy aromas swirl and race,
With roots that laugh, a delightful place.
In my kitchen, a wild, fragrant spree,
Turns into a comedy, just watch and see!

Foliage's Soft Embrace

Ferns are dancing in the breeze,
They're happy, if you please.
A squirrel slipped on some dew,
And giggled in his tiny shoe.

The daisies wore their silly hats,
While butterflies played acrobats.
The ivy climbs with goofy glee,
As if it drew a smiley tree.

Potted plants hold tea parties,
With jolly frogs in tiny T-shirts.
But the cactus pricked the donuts dry,
And laughed while wearing a strawberry tie.

So come and join this leafy cheer,
With puns and plants to share a beer.
In this garden, grins align,
Nature's humor tastes divine!

Lanterns of Light in the Leafy Nook

In the corner of the yard,
A pumpkin glows and plays the bard.
It tells tall tales to the sun,
Of mischievous tricks and silly fun.

The daisies whisper to the clouds,
While wicked weeds form silly crowds.
They planned a party, oh so grand,
And picked a worm to be the band.

The light bulbs wear their brightest hues,
While fireflies dance in polka shoes.
A toad croaks out his favorite tune,
While crickets hum beneath the moon.

Join the laughter in this nook,
Where every leaf's a joyful book.
With lanterns lit and spirits high,
Even the shadows cosplay and fly!

Bowery of Bountiful Breaths

In the bowery where laughter roams,
A catnap's worth of leafy homes.
The cucumbers wear party hats,
While radishes dance with floppy bats.

Mint and basil have a chat,
Comparing who smells best, imagine that!
But mint sneezed, and oh dear me,
An aroma war broke out like confetti.

The tomatoes turned into balloons,
While peas tried kayaking with spoons.
A beet claimed it was a hotshot,
And danced like a star in a veggie pot.

So take a breath amongst the greens,
Where fun erupts in leafy scenes.
Nature giggles, never ceases,
In this garden full of breezy pieces!

The Dance of the Dappled Sunlight

Underneath the leafy play,
Sunlight twinkles, bright as day.
The shadows plot a sillier act,
While squirrels rehearse their comedy pact.

The daisies twirl in their flowery skirts,
As beetles bumble, avoiding their flirts.
Sunbeams yell, "Let's brighten the scene!"
And the branches swayed like a dance machine.

The apples jived with every giggle,
While grasshoppers made the crowd wiggle.
A leaf dropped down, it felt a breeze,
Landing on the stage with style and ease.

So come and join this bright parade,
With laughter as the music played.
In dappled light, we all find joy,
In this garden where we can deploy!

The Lush Symphony of Nature

In the garden, squirrels dance,
With acorns tucked in each little pants.
The flowers sing a cheeky tune,
While bees buzz round like a bustling moon.

The grass tickles toes in delight,
As lizards practice their stand-up night.
The daisies giggle, the tulips tease,
Nature's comedians bring us to our knees.

Lawn chairs filled with folks in shade,
Judging tomatoes on the parade.
A chorus of frogs with crickets in tow,
Serenading under the moon's soft glow.

The trees wave leaves in frivolous cheer,
While ants march on like they have no fear.
Nature here cracks jokes without a care,
In the lush symphony that fills the air.

Eden at the Heart of the Earth

Amidst the flora, there's quite the scene,
Bunnies hopping like they're on a routine.
The worms wriggle, a slippery troupe,
A muddy party under the leafy hoop.

Birds feature in a karaoke fight,
Chirping covers of tunes both day and night.
A bee drops in for a taste of gossip,
While sunflowers flaunt a tall, proud posture.

Ladybugs wearing spots like a dress,
Strut their stuff, they know they're the best.
Petunias giggle with their fragrant flair,
As ants tell tales of the snacks they dare.

In this garden, the fun's never ceased,
With laughter and mischief in nature's feast.
Each plant a comedian and critters in jest,
Life blooms here, it's simply the best!

Serene Hues of Hibernation

The bears snore loud, what a funny sound,
As they dream of fish in the snowy ground.
The trees wear scarves made of frosty dew,
While critters tuneful serenade the view.

Under blankets of white, life takes a nap,
Squirrels wrapped tight in a cozy flap.
The snowflakes giggle, they're falling fast,
As frostbitten flowers look aghast.

A penguin slides with an awkward flair,
While winter greens toss their chilly hair.
The wise old owl hoots the night away,
As critters plan their next holiday.

Hibernation brings a comical chill,
The laughter of winter, a sweet little thrill.
As nature sleeps, the jokes may pause,
But spring will come, and we'll laugh with applause!

The Canopy's Gentle Lullaby

In the treetops, the monkeys swing,
With tail acrobatics that make us grin.
The parrots squawk in a colorful race,
Chasing sunshine all over the place.

Below, the sloths take their time,
Climbing slow, like it's some grand crime.
While the orchids whisper jokes so sly,
Petals shaking like they're laughing high.

The vines weave stories in twisty loops,
As playful foxes chase after the troops.
Frogs in the pond share their best puns,
While the sun waves goodbye to the evening runs.

Nature's canopy holds secrets untold,
Jokes carved in bark, brave and bold.
With laughter ringing from dawn to dusk,
The wild welcomes all in its leafy husk.

Nestled in Nature's Arms

In a nook with plants galore,
The cat gave chase to a leaf by the door.
I tripped over pots, what a sight,
Who knew a fern could put up a fight!

The cactus waved as I walked by,
'No hugs for me, just a friendly hi!'
I talk to the ivy, it's no big fuss,
It rolls its leaves, quite a curious plus.

Sunshine spills in, the air is sweet,
A jungle gym for my playful feet.
The blooms gossip, I swear they do,
'Watch out for that rogue, the rogue gnome too!'

And when the rain gives a light tap,
The plants dance on, no need for a map.
Laughter sprouts from every corner,
In my abode, nature's a performer!

Flourishing Corners of Comfort

In the corner, herbs whisper their dreams,
While daisies giggle in sunlit beams.
A rubber plant's got quite the attitude,
I swear it rolls its eyes, what a shrewd dude!

The sofa's swallowed by the lush vines,
Can't find the remote, oh how it pines!
A succulent's plotting a hitchhike spree,
Off to the windowsill, feeling quite free!

Pothos and peace lilies hold a debate,
'Tell me, who's the prettiest here — don't wait!'
I sip my tea, oh what a scene,
A comedy show, where no one's mean!

And just when I think it's time to rest,
The rubber plant shouts, 'We've not had our best!'
So we dance and laugh, my leafy friends,
Life's sweet as honey when nature pretends!

Boughs and Blooms Beneath Our Roof

Under boughs that bend and sway,
A chorus of colors brightens the day.
A gnome on a tricycle rolls by with flair,
As marigolds chuckle, teasing the air.

The orchids wear gowns of velvet delight,
While ferns wiggle in sheer, leafy flight.
Together they plot a green masquerade,
Joking 'bout leaves that have slightly frayed.

A sunflower thinks it's the star of the room,
While I chase a beetle who thinks he can zoom.
Amidst this chaos, joy intertwines,
A party of plants, with no need for wines!

So if you drop by, take a look around,
Boughs and blooms, what fun to be found!
Nature's a clown, here in my space,
Where laughter and green share a warm embrace!

The Serenity of Swaying Leaves

In the wind, the leaves perform a jig,
While I sip tea, doing a little wig.
The trees peek in, all curious and sly,
As I look up, 'Hey there, don't be shy!'

A dainty sprout steals the scene with a twirl,
'Hey, watch me dance!' it gives a little whirl.
The sunbeams giggle as shadows play,
What a setup for a green cabaret!

The crickets chirp, it's a rhythmic song,
Nature's orchestra, can't go wrong!
Even the weeds have their moments in tow,
'You know we're trendy, just watch us grow!'

And so the day fades, but here's the truth,
Serenity blooms, there's joy in my youth.
While leaves sway gently, a whimsical tease,
I find my happiness beneath these trees!

Breaths of Fresh Earth

The garden's alive with a quirky flair,
Even the weeds have begun to declare.
A dandelion parade, look at them prance,
With a jig and a wiggle, they all take a chance.

The cucumbers whisper, 'We're in a pickle!'
While tomatoes giggle, the jokes are quite fickle.
A cabbage rolls over and snores quite loud,
While the lettuce performs for a giggling crowd.

The carrots are plotting a silly surprise,
To jump out of the ground and dazzle our eyes.
With bugs as their buddies, they dance through the dirt,
Laughing at moles who just might get hurt.

So let's toss some seeds in this land of delight,
Join the ruckus, squeeze in, hold on tight!
For in every corner and patch we reclaim,
Lies a chuckle and joy, with nature to blame.

Blossoms, Buds, and Beyond

The tulips are gossiping, bright as can be,
While daisies are blending in jests, can't you see?
The roses are bragging about their perfume,
While the daisies protest, 'We're up to the bloom!'

In a daffodil dance, a joyous affair,
The bees wear tuxedos—what a charming pair!
With each little buzz, they say cheeky things,
Like 'Pollen is bliss' while they flaunt their wings.

A sunflower snoozes, comically tall,
Bending to share in the laughter of all.
The petals keep poking, and all of them tease,
'We're the jests of the garden, brought down to our knees!'

Under bright skies, there's silliness galore,
Where blossoms and buds always want to explore.
They spread joy and chuckles, just wait for the show,
In the wildest of colors, in nature's tableau.

Pondering Among Petals

Amidst the petals, a conundrum unfolds,
Why do flowers wear shoes that are covered in mold?
The daisies debate on just which side is best,
While the marigolds grin, enjoying the quest.

What do butterflies wear for a night out on town?
Imagine the outfits—what a colorful gown!
The bees buzz along, all matchy so bright,
Shouting, 'We're fabulous—oh what a sight!'

The bumblebees fry up an odd pancake treat,
While the lilies all giggle, 'That's hard to eat!'
With a sprinkle of humor, the garden's aglow,
As petals keep pondering what's next in the show.

As the moon casts a glow, the fun won't exhaust,
In whispers among petals, there's not much that's lost.
Laughing through thorns, the blossoms abide,
In this silly oasis, where curiosities ride.

The Canvas of Climbing Vines

The vines are all tangled in a whimsical dance,
They're arguing over who leads the prance.
'No me!' says the ivy, while the beans snicker loud,
'You're all just confused, let's go join the crowd!'

A trellis declares it a temporary throne,
While the tomatoes shout, 'Let's not leave it alone!'
With laughter and giggles, they weave and they climb,
Creating a circus that's truly sublime.

The gourds pout and sulk, feeling left out,
'We simply can't reach, there's too much doubt!'
The chickpeas chime in, 'Just grow and be free!'
And forget about barriers like we do with glee.

So behold this canvas of verdant delight,
Where laughter and antics take flight every night.
In the arms of the sun, they twist and they crawl,
These climbing creations just want to enthrall.

Sunlit Corners of the Growing Space

In the sunlit nook, a plant sneezes,
Its leafy friends giggle in the breezes.
Cacti wear shades, looking so cool,
While ferns play chess, acting like fools.

Roses are gossiping, sharing their blooms,
While daisies breakdance, clearing the room.
Lettuce is chuckling, just can't hold it in,
Saying, "I'm crunchy, but still full of sin!"

Basil's cooking up a fragrant delight,
Says, "I'm the herb that makes everything right!"
Tomatoes are tumbling, rolling for fun,
Declaring, "All veggies deserve a good run!"

In the corner, a succulent's sprawled out,
Confidently lounging with nary a doubt.
If leaves had voices, what tales they would weave,
In this merry space where they all believe!

The Flora-Filled Refuge

In a refuge of greens, the party has begun,
Where petunias moonwalk and orchids just run.
Ferns flip pancakes, oh what a sight,
While daisies try karaoke late into the night.

Bamboo's a DJ, spinning tunes with flair,
Lettuce joins in, tossing seeds in the air.
The violets are giggling, doing the twist,
Saying, "This bash is a flora-filled tryst!"

Basil holds court, ruling with zest,
While rosemary's playing the game of chess best.
Thyme throws a party in the soil so deep,
With roots dancing merrily, not losing their sleep.

If plants could laugh, oh what joy they would find,
In this flora-filled refuge, so wonderfully kind!
Let's toast to the greens, the laughs here unfurl,
In our quirky oasis, an emerald swirl!

Melodies of Moss and Meadow

In the melodies sung by the moss and the glade,
Frogs croak in harmony, serenading the shade.
Butterflies dance in a colorful spree,
As daisies twirl about just like fairy-trees.

Grasshoppers join in, tapping their feet,
While toads play the drums, keeping the beat.
The wind whispers secrets through leaves overhead,
Singing sweet songs to every flowerbed.

Meadows of laughter, sunshine, and cheer,
Even the weeds join in without fear!
Together they giggle, plants all aglow,
In this wild concert where craziness flows.

If only the world could witness this show,
Where nature's the star, putting on quite the glow!
With notes made of green, and beats made of dew,
Melodies echo in this vibrant view!

Vibrant Spirits Beneath the Boughs

Beneath the great boughs, the spirits abound,
Where gossiping leaves share tales all around.
The acorns have laughter, rolling with glee,
Squirrels join in, planning a heist for some free.

In the shade of the oak, a party takes flight,
Where mushrooms play charades, all silly delight.
Fungi are giggling, dancing with flair,
While brambles throw confetti high in the air.

The branches are swaying, keeping the beat,
Pinecones are partying, isn't that neat?
With sunlight like sprinkles, the day's such a treat,
Nature's a showman, can't admit defeat!

So toast to the roots and the greenery bold,
Where vibrant spirits never grow old.
In this world of laughter, magic unfolds,
Beneath the great boughs, a story retold!

Secrets Beneath the Canopy

Under leaves, the squirrels tease,
With acorn plans, they do as they please.
Their chatter sounds like tiny debates,
While ants march by with snack-filled plates.

Beneath the boughs, a rabbit's waltz,
He's got moves that sprout from faults.
The owls hoot in a comic way,
As if to join the wild ballet.

Caterpillars wear their best attire,
They strut like models, never tire.
But when a breeze gives them chills,
They hide away, afraid of thrills.

With secrets shared in giggles and glee,
The trees keep whispers, wild and free.
Nature's jesters with their antics grand,
Remind us all to laugh, unplanned.

Nature's Cozy Embrace

In the garden, a gnome does smile,
With a beard sprouting like a green mile.
He nods at flowers, claims them his kin,
While butterflies invade, with flutters akin.

Chickens gossip about the best seeds,
Clucking advice for all of their needs.
With pecking and prancing, they strut about,
In this feathery tale, there's never a doubt.

A hedgehog hiccups, a funny sight,
While raccoons dance in the soft moonlight.
With twirls and dives, their rhythm is strong,
Nature's own band, where all can belong.

Beneath the sky, where laughter reigns,
Every creature knows, joy never wanes.
In this cozy nook of silly delight,
Nature chuckles softly, a true delight.

Leafy Retreats and Tranquil Streets

The trees in line wear hats of green,
Like stylish folks, they preen and glean.
With branches waving, they cheer us on,
"Keep it light, just dance till dawn!"

The flowers gossip, oh what a sight,
"Did you see that bee? He thinks he's so bright!"
They giggle and sway with every breeze,
Creating a buzz with effortless ease.

A snail in a shell takes the slowest stroll,
While frogs on lily pads rock and roll.
They croak out jokes, quite absurd and bold,
In this leafy haven, tales of old.

Leafy retreats where silliness grows,
Where every turn a new tale flows.
With laughter bubbling under canopies wide,
In nature's embrace, we all can abide.

Hues of Life in Every Nook

In a patch of sun, a curious cat,
Prowls about, in pursuit of a rat.
But finds a butterfly, and gets quite coy,
"Forget the chase, this is pure joy!"

The earthworms wiggle in their party suits,
While ladybugs dance in tiny, sleek boots.
Together they plan grand celebrations,
With confetti leaves and wild imitations.

Pine cones roll like little hats,
With pine needle spikes—what a look for cats!
They prance and parade through the grassy show,
In this vibrant world, antics do flow.

In every nook, a splash of delight,
From buzzing bees to bugs taking flight.
With hues so vivid, it's surely a boon,
In this merry realm, we all feel in tune.

Secrets of the Verdant Shelter

In the corners, ferns hold court,
They gossip secrets, of an old tort.
A cat named Jasper, in a sunbeam lies,
Dreaming of fish, under bright blue skies.

The snail in his shell, thinks he's so wise,
While ants plan parties, behind his eyes.
The sunflower nods, with a silly grin,
Says, 'Join the dance, let the fun begin!'

Potted herbs sing, in pots piled high,
Mint tells the rosemary, 'You're a pie!'
With laughter and leaves, the space feels grand,
It's a leafy circus, at hand of hand.

Caterpillars wiggle, with fluffy flair,
As ladybugs judge, with a fancy air.
Come join the feast, of twirls and spins,
In a world of green, mischief begins!

Home Among the Shadows and the Sun

In the bright beams, shadows play,
As grasshoppers leap, in their quirky ballet.
Lemonade puddles, underfoot squish,
While frogs practice songs, with a resounding swish.

The daisies gossip, about the day's catch,
While snickering mosses prepare for a match.
A squirrel in haste, drops acorns galore,
And claims he's a chef—what a nutty chore!

The breeze carries laughter, from flower to tree,
As butterflies flaunt, 'Ain't life carefree?'
With shadows and sun, each petal's a jest,
In a garden of giggles, they plant the best.

A woodpecker laughs at his clumsy routine,
While lilies roll over, in shades of green.
Join in the fun, for it's all just a show,
This whimsical patch, where giggles grow!

Pathways of Petals and Peace

Along the path, where daisies confide,
There's a bunny who prances, full of pride.
He flips and he flops, with no cares at all,
Declaring, 'Let's party, let's have a ball!'

The tulips throw shade, as they sway to the beat,
While a hedgehog brings snacks, quite a tasty treat.
With each little giggle, the petals take flight,
As bees in the background, buzz with delight.

A puppy bounds in, with mud on his nose,
He sniffs out the fun, in colorful clothes.
Together they whirl, in a dance of the bliss,
In this pathway of petals, who could resist?

Each step is a story, of laughter and play,
In the joy of the moment, let worries decay.
With friends all around, let's frolic and roam,
For laughter blooms bright, in this patch we call home!

Each Leaf a Memory's Whisper

In the breeze, leaves chuckle, full of tales,
About flying kites, and epic fails.
The maple sways, like a grand old friend,
Whispering secrets, that never do end.

A squirrel with antics, all out of place,
Finding acorns, that run in a race.
The ivy chuckles, 'I've seen it all,
From creeping to climbing, for me it's a ball!'

Dandelions grinning, a fierce little crew,
Blowing their wishes, where wishes come true.
And every soft rustle, a tickle of cheer,
In this leafy lounge, where worries disappear.

With each leaf a memory, the laughter ignites,
Brewing up stories, on warm starry nights.
In the maze of the greens, join in the fun,
For every sweet whisper, is a dance begun!

Where Roots and Resilience Flourish

In the corner, a plant dons a hat,
Moving in rhythm, it thinks it's a cat.
With leaves that sway, it holds the floor,
One day it may even knock on the door.

The cactus grins, spikes all a-dance,
Calling the fern for a twirling romance.
Together they plot their horticultural fame,
With dreams of a garden that leads to a game.

The herbs in the kitchen, a jive in the pot,
Basil and parsley preparing a plot.
They whisper secrets of flavor and zest,
While the thyme in the corner just can't help but jest.

And when the sun sets, they all gather 'round,
Telling tall tales, some lost then found.
With giggles and snickers, the laughter takes flight,
In this leafy haven that buzzes with light.

Canopy Conversations in the Calm

Beneath the leaves, where whispers abound,
A squirrel rehearses a stand-up sound.
He jokes about nuts and the acorns' plight,
While the trees chuckle, swaying left and right.

The flowers gossip, trading bright tips,
About the bees' dances and pollen-swaps flips.
They blush in their colors, a vibrant parade,
While the daisies dive into sunbathing shade.

Amidst the branches, a clever old crow,
Narrates the tale of a gardening show.
With sun-hats and shovels, the critters all cheer,
As funny mishaps bring harmony near.

So come take a peek at their leafy affair,
You'll leave with a grin, and fresh forest air.
In this charming garden, laughter won't cease,
With nature's chatter, they're crafting their peace.

Hearth of the Hearty Kale

In the pot, the kale does a little dance,
Challenging lettuce to take a chance.
With a twirl and a hop, it claims the crown,
While spinach just sighs, feeling a bit brown.

The garlic joins in with a bold little twist,
Saying, "Don't forget, we make quite the hit!"
As onions cry out, "It's the flavor we bring,
Together we make the veggies all sing!"

Chopping board symphonies fill up the space,
As carrots compete for the brightest face.
With laughter and crunches, they'll serve up a dish,
A colorful medley, everyone's wish.

And when they are served, it's a veggie delight,
With giggles and grins shared over each bite.
Who knew a garden could be such a scene?
Where food brings the jokes, and flavors are keen!

The Color of Contentment

In the sun, the grass wears a cheeky green coat,
As frogs leap about, singing songs on a boat.
With a splash and a croak, the show's underway,
While daisies blush pink at their merry ballet.

The sunflowers wink, with petals like rays,
Waving their arms in the light-hearted plays.
They gossip about where the bees made their trip,
And who's getting favorite blooms from the trip.

In the shed, the gnomes are plotting a game,
Betting on which plant will earn the most fame.
With laughter and banter, they pave their own way,
In this garden of joy, where worries decay.

So raise your glass to this riotous scene,
Where laughter takes root in everything green.
Join in the fun of this cultivated glee,
In the garden of life, let your spirit run free!

Hues of Hearth and Herb

When the plants start to dance,
They know just what to do,
They sway with glee to the music,
While I trip on a shoe.

My basil has a best friend,
A pot of thyme, you see,
They chat about the weather,
While I sip my mint tea.

The ferns hold secret meetings,
In shadows, they conspire,
Planning how to take over,
Our neighbor's garden choir.

And when the sun runs away,
The daisies play charades,
But I'm looking for a snack,
And I find a few charades.

A Treetop Talisman

My tree outside has wisdom,
It tells the passing cars,
They slow down to listen softly,
To the gossip of the stars.

The squirrels throw a wild party,
With acorns they can share,
I peek from my window sill,
Wishing I could be a bear.

A raccoon snuck in for dinner,
He stole my leftover fries,
Now every time I hear rustling,
I jump and check the pies.

If trees could tell their secrets,
They'd probably sing out loud,
Of creatures in my backyard,
And the chaos of the crowd.

Cultivated Corners of Comfort

In the corner—broccoli cheers,
Carrots are on strike,
They want to play the piano,
Instead of taste on a bike.

The tomatoes plot their romance,
With onions as the match,
I left them for a moment,
They're now a tangled batch.

Cacti hold the best advice,
They say, "Stay sharp and bright!"
But I can't quite grasp their wisdom,
I'm too busy overbite.

And lettuce loves the gossip,
Crunchy as a laughing tease,
I'll join their leafy chatter,
As I munch on my cheese.

The Greenhouse of My Heart

In my heart, a jungle thrives,
With vines that twirl and twist,
I often lose my favorite sock,
    Amongst that leafy mist.

The peas are binge-watching sitcoms,
While parsley takes the lead,
They laugh so loud; my neighbors say,
    "What vegan lives in greed?"

The mint leaves throw a rave,
With flavors made to sway,
While I just roll on by,
And celebrate with hay.

So here I am, grinning wide,
In this green, quirky zone,
Where nature gives a wink or two,
    And I'm never alone.

Whispers of Verdant Corners

In corners where the ferns all laugh,
The cat slips by on a leafy path.
A spider spins a web of jokes,
While lazy plants trade sleepy pokes.

The chili plants throw spicy fits,
While daisies wiggle, showing their bits.
The succulents gossip about the sun,
As the watering can joins in the fun.

A lizard dances on the stone,
With tiny moves, he's in the zone.
The fern begins to shake and sway,
To join the merry, plant parade!

In this chaos of petals and leaves,
Even the ants wear tiny sleeves.
A hammock hums a dreamy tune,
In this jungle, all is marooned.

Sanctuary of Lush Dreams

In this jungle of mismatched socks,
Where houseplants play polite knocks.
The rubber tree makes a grand demand,
For more sunlight, and a helping hand.

The monstera whispers secrets bold,
While the dust bunnies dare not be told.
Each leaf has quirks, critiques to share,
It's a leafy soap opera, so rare!

The bird sings loudly, a karaoke star,
As the cactus throws parties from afar.
With laughter floating through the air,
These tangled greens are beyond compare!

Amidst the ferns in bright display,
The watering can joins the fray.
With giggles sprouting all around,
In this haven, joy abounds!

Emerald Embrace

Among the greens, a snail's slow race,
And every plant has its own face.
The ivy teases with a sly grin,
While the pansies giggle, pulling him in.

The tomato plant wears a crown,
Claiming royalty, never a frown.
Her fruit drips laughter, salsa delight,
While the beans dance under the starlight.

The shady nook hums a tune,
While the potting soil claims the moon.
"Who needs curtains?" the ferns do say,
With their arms flailing, the fun's on display!

Even the weeds have stories to share,
In this merry world, all is fair.
With every leaf, the comedy unfolds,
In emerald joy, the heart beholds!

The Garden's Gentle Heart

In the garden's heart, there's quite the show,
Where rhubarb knows it steals the glow.
The sunflowers twirl with floppy heads,
While ants hold parades, in lines like threads.

Each sprout feels bold, and wildly chic,
The garden gnome wonders, "Is that a sneak?"
The marigolds hum a buzzing tune,
While the weeds giggle beneath the moon.

A frog in the fountain tries a hand,
At stand-up comedy, oh so grand.
The daisies snicker at every quip,
As dragonflies join for a little flip!

In this patchwork of winks and blooms,
Every corner's ripe with giggling fumes.
With every leaf, a pun takes flight,
Here's to laughter and garden delight!

The Silent Growth of Togetherness

In corners where the vines entwine,
We trip on roots, it's quite divine.
The cat thinks she's a leafy queen,
While we star in this leafy scene.

The fridge is filled with kale and glee,
We munch on greens like rabbits, see!
Yet still, the pizza's call is loud,
Our salad's lost in veggie shroud.

The sprouts talk back with sassy flair,
They gossip about our messy hair.
Each pot whispers of dreams untold,
As we laugh, it never gets old.

Together we grow, in jest and cheer,
Our hearts bloom bright without a fear.
Who knew that veggies brought such fun?
A family bond that's never done!

Embraced by Nature's Tenderness

I stepped outside, a wave of green,
Bees zipping past, what a scene!
Dancing flowers swayed with glee,
I think they might be tipsy, see?

The dog dug deep for treasure's stake,
Unveiled a plant instead of cake.
He shrugged it off, a muddy mess,
While the plants giggled, I confess.

My neighbor's lawn, it grows with pride,
But ours looks like it's on a slide.
He grins with envy, I can't deny,
As dandelions wave goodbye.

The sun beams down, so warm and bright,
Nature's hugs bring pure delight.
In our quirky yard, life's a show,
With laughs galore, we steal the flow!

The Garden's Gentle Guardians

The gnomes are watching, eyes so bold,
With tiny smiles, their tales unfold.
But when the moon shines, they plot and scheme,
To dance around like in a dream.

The snails glide by in glimmers slow,
They take their time, and it does show.
In this parade of leafy fun,
We're all just playing, no need to run.

Mice munch berries with secret glee,
While squirrels steal our plans, you see?
Each garden foe and friend imbued,
Makes nature's stage a merry mood.

With tender care, we keep the peace,
Among this chaos, love won't cease.
In every pot, there's laughter glowed,
In this green realm, we feel bestowed!

Hues of Harmony in the Heart

The purple blooms wave, 'Hello!' so bright,
While orange marigolds argue at night.
The daisies laugh with sheer delight,
In our chaotic floral fight.

Each leaf reflects our silly ways,
In messy moments, joy displays.
We paint the garden with giggles and sprays,
As sunbeams twinkle and softly blaze.

The funny bugs parade with pride,
In mismatched stripes, they coincide.
At twilight's blush, they twirl and twine,
A dance that feels simply divine.

With colors bright, and smiles that soar,
We share our hearts, forevermore.
In this vibrant space, our spirits climb,
In harmony's hues, we rhyme and chime!

Ephemeral Tendrils of Growth

Once a sprout did squash my heart,
It grew so fast, I had to part.
Teased by leaves, it danced with glee,
Now it's taller than me!

Potted plants threw quite the bash,
Cactus wore shades, a total splash.
Fern forgets the sun so bright,
Whispers jokes in the moonlight.

In this jungle, I'm the prey,
Lost my socks, but it's okay.
Those vines snicker, do they know?
They've got me tangled in their show!

With a wink and leafy spin,
Every wilting flower's grin.
Who needs soil for a good time?
Let's rhyme funny with a climb!

The Comfort of Climbing Vines

Those vines are climbing up the wall,
Like they're trying to win a brawl.
Twisting 'round my favorite chair,
Do they think I'm cool to share?

I found one weeding out my snacks,
Rummaging through my chips and packs.
"Hey!" I shouted, "That's not fair!"
It wrapped around, as if to swear.

The curtains blush with lovely greens,
Laughter hidden in their sheens.
With every climb, I start to rise,
Until I trip, oh what a surprise!

So here I sit with plants in tow,
Plant sips tea and starts to glow.
Who knew a vine could crack a pun?
Nature surely knows how to have fun!

Essence of the Emerald Retreat

In a corner where green leaves twirl,
Sits a snail, a very slow girl.
She curls around a dandy vine,
Whispering secrets, oh so fine.

A plant once stole my favorite hat,
It wore it proudly, imagine that!
Every cactus struck a pose,
While blossoms giggled, in rows they rose.

Mossy carpets beneath my feet,
Each step forward feels like a feat.
I asked the daisies for a clue,
"Steal a line and escape too!"

The garden swings like a big, green joke,
Swaying gently, invoking smoke.
I'll burst with laughter, that's my plan,
In this cozy, leafy span!

Serenity Amidst the Evergreens

Evergreens wave like they own the place,
While squirrels act with sheer grace.
They chuckle at my clumsy ways,
I curtsy, but they don't even gaze.

A pinecone dropped, it smacked my head,
Is this why the forest said?
"Watch your step while you explore,
Lumberjack's jokes are never a bore!"

Beneath the shade, I find serenity,
With leaf-shaped laughter, oh, the glee!
I invite the trees to join my dance,
But they're stuck in a leafy trance.

So here I sit, roots in delight,
Cracking jokes from morning till night.
In this thicket where chuckles reign,
Evergreens giggle, loving the gain!

Life's Breath through Branching Shadows

Under the leafy cover, we play,
A squirrel on a mission, gone astray.
Twisting through branches, we laugh and cheer,
Chasing the shadows, never show fear.

Mosquitoes the size of tiny drones,
Conducting a concert of buzzing tones.
But with a swat and a comical dance,
We giggle together, give fate a chance.

The breeze sings a tune, fresh like a dream,
While grass tickles toes, or so it may seem.
A picnic of mishaps and crumbs everywhere,
Who's responsible? Let's not make it clear!

So under the canopy, off we traverse,
Nature's great stage, a hilarious verse.
With each branch we bump, oh how we'll tease,
In this green wonderland, we do as we please.

A Tapestry of Treetops

Branches are bowing, painting the sky,
As apples pretend they might just fly by.
A monkey's a neighbor, or maybe a ghost,
In this leafy realm, we gather and boast.

With acorns for hats and leaves like capes,
We prance and we dance, making silly shapes.
The wind joins our laughter, a playful guide,
Through this forest maze, an adventure wide.

Raccoons peek in with their curious eyes,
As we plan our escape with mischievous sighs.
"Who brought the snacks?" is the question of the day,
But they vanished like magic, much to our dismay.

Yet here in the trees, we're never alone,
With laughter so bright, we've created our zone.
A fabric of giggles, nature's bright seam,
In this tapestry of treetops, we dream.

Home is Where the Greenheart Blooms

Where the daisies are giggling, and roses play tag,
Where weeds hold court on the lilypad rag.
We dance with the daisies, take turns with the bees,
In this jungle of jokes, oh what a tease!

Thistles throw shade, but we're too busy grinning,
A toss of bright petals, and that's just the beginning.
Butterflies flutter like confetti in flight,
In this garden of madness, everything's right.

The grass blades create a delightful scene,
Tickling our ankles, they're super serene.
"A race to the fountain!" we shout with delight,
But slip on a slug, oh what a funny sight!

Handfuls of laughter and bouquets of cheer,
In this riot of colors, it's clear we are near.
With roots intertwined, we're tangled in glee,
In this place full of blooms, all wild and free.

The Whispering Grass Beneath Our Feet

In fields of tall whispers, we skip with grace,
With blades that tell secrets, a murmurous place.
We drop down for laughter, rolling in glee,
While ants plot their takeover, smart as can be.

The daisies are gossiping, sharing their tales,
"A butterfly flitted!" Oh, how it prevails!
We mimic the buzzing, pretending to fly,
With arms like wings, we soar to the sky.

The grass tickles toes, while the wind makes us sway,
With giggles and wiggles, we chase woes away.
Oh look, here comes Mom, with snacks from the past,
"Here's a feast for the brave!" Now, who's first to fast?

So here in this laughter, beneath all the cheer,
In fields where the grass whispers, love draws us near.
With each silly moment, we feel quite complete,
In this riot of green, life's funny and sweet.

Sprouts of Joy in Every Room

In the kitchen, herbs conspire,
To spice the soup, a leafy choir.
Basil winks, while parsley laughs,
As garlic rolls on greenish paths.

In the living room, succulents dance,
Cacti poke, taking a chance.
Fern flips its fronds to the beat,
While lilies shuffle on tiny feet.

The bathroom hosts a mossy throne,
Where bathroom plants feel not alone.
They gossip by the bubble bath,
Sharing secrets with a laugh.

In every nook, laughter's green,
A quirky vibe, a leafy scene.
With every sprout, joy takes its flight,
A giggle here, a chuckle bright.

Treetops Telling Tales

Beneath the oak, we gather round,
Tree limbs sway, they share their sounds.
"Once I sprouted, just a twig,
Now I'm tall, I dance a jig!"

The maple chimes with vibrant hues,
"Oh, let me tell of mushroom blues!
In springtime rain, we'd stomp and play,
Letting squishy dirt get in the way!"

The pine throws down a needle's joke,
"Ever try a needle poke?
But in the breeze, I'm quite the king,
Hop on my back, let's spread our wings!"

With laughter branching far and wide,
Nature's humor fills the ride.
In the canopy, tales unfold,
Funny stories that we hold.

Roommates with Roots

In the hallway, plants reside,
Sharing tips on how to glide.
"Hey there, succulent, what's the key?
To be so cool, and still so free?"

The fern replies with a floppy wave,
"Just soak it up, don't be a slave!
A little sun, a drink or two,
You'll find your groove, just like we do."

The pothos climbs the stairway wall,
"Who needs rooms? I'll take them all!"
While spider plants dangle with flair,
Offering their wild hair with care.

With potting soil and cheery glee,
We're all roommates in this crazy spree.
Rooting for each other in sunlight's embrace,
A family of leaves in this wild space.

Chasing Shadows in the Foliage

In the garden, shadows prance,
Beneath each leaf, we take a chance.
A butterfly's laugh, a worm's old joke,
Life's a circus, and we're the folk.

The daisies wink, "We've seen it all,
From clumsy bees to the fence that's tall.
Chasing shadows, oh what a sight,
Keeping secrets 'til the night."

The tomato grins, "I'm red and round,
But in the dirt, I'm glory-bound.
Every twist and turn's a game,
Who knew sunlight could bring such fame?"

As we chase those bright distractions,
Nature brings its own attractions.
Underneath the leafy chance,
We laugh and twirl in leafy dance.

www.ingramcontent.com/pod-product-compliance
Lightning Source LLC
Chambersburg PA
CBHW072123070526
44585CB00016B/1538